To Love As We Are Loved

To Love As We Are Loved

The Bible and Relationships

BRUCE C. BIRCH

ABINGDON PRESS / Nashville

TO LOVE AS WE ARE LOVED
THE BIBLE AND RELATIONSHIPS

Copyright © 1992 by Abingdon Press

This book is printed on acid-free, recycled paper.

Library of Congress Cataloging-in-Publication Data

Birch, Bruce C.
    To love as we are loved : the Bible and relationships / Bruce C.
Birch.
        p.   cm.
    ISBN 0-687-42188-8 (alk. paper)
    1. Interpersonal relations—Religious aspects—Christianity. 2.
Interpersonal relations—Biblical teaching.   I. Title.
BV4597.52.B56   1992
233—dc20   92-13016
                                                         CIP

All scripture quotations, except for brief paraphrases or unless
otherwise noted, are from the New Revised Standard Version of the
Bible, copyright © 1989 by the Division of Christian Education of
the National Council of the Churches of Christ in the United States
of America, and are used by permission.

Scripture quotations noted RSV are from the Revised Standard
Version of the Bible, copyright 1946, 1952, 1971 by the Division of
Christian Education of the National Council of Churches of Christ
in the U.S.A. and are used by permission.

MANUFACTURED IN THE UNITED STATES OF AMERICA

CONTENTS

PREFACE

*T*he essays in this book originated as Bible studies done for the National Conference on Human Sexuality Education sponsored by the Board of Discipleship of The United Methodist Church and held in Nashville on April 9–12, 1989. I was asked to introduce each morning with a Bible study that would help give focus to the wide range of issues to be dealt with in the conference.

As I thought about this task it became clear to me that the Bible does not abstract human sexuality from the wider concerns of human relationship. I chose not to focus on what the Bible says about this or that issue but to focus on how our human relationships, including our sexuality, are modeled by God's relationship to us. It was my desire to set the concern for particular issues into a broader framework of a biblical theology of relationship. The results are encompassed in these essays.

I have resisted the impulse to expand these pieces into a scholarly treatise. I have not added footnotes; I have edited the material so that it sounds a little less like speeches and reads more easily. But my hope is that the essays have retained the simple, direct quality of their original purpose: to provide a biblical grounding for our thinking about relationships, not only in the sexual dimension where we struggle with a number of difficult issues, but in all those aspects of human relationships that form the circumstances of our lives. If the use of these essays in the church simply stimulates us to reflect more thoughtfully on how our biblical faith makes a difference in the relationships of our lives, then the book will have served its purpose.

I want to express my thanks to Celia Beam, who organized the Nashville conference and invited me to do the Bible studies. I am very grateful to Neil M. Alexander and Ronald P. Patterson of Abingdon Press for encouraging publication of these essays and guiding them through the process. I am indebted to my friend and colleague Carroll Saussy for reading this material and offering some very helpful suggestions.

To Love
As We Are
Loved

CHAPTER 1

Relationship as Freedom

O̲ur relationship to God comes to us, in the testimony of the biblical witnesses, as a freely given gift. We are called into relationship by the freely given grace of God. We have the possibility of meaningful interaction with others as a gift and not as a duty. We make free choices about relationships, rather than relate by instinctual pattern like other animals. Thus, we were created for relationship to one another in freedom.

This is not our customary way of thinking about relationships. We are more prone to think in terms of duties, prescribed roles, customs, or laws. Most of the time we don't think about it at all; we just *fall* into the available patterns. We seldom think of relationship as a freely given gift, first from God and then of each to the other, and this is *especially* true in the area of human sexuality. Perhaps there is no other aspect of our relationships to one another that is more often constricted by accepted and prescribed roles, patterns, duties, customs, and laws. It's sometimes simply easier to accept these prescriptions, and to allow them to make decisions for us, than to consciously call up any critical categories for moral understanding or decision making about our relationships.

It is for that reason that we need to reclaim once again the quality of God's freedom as essential to our relationship to God, and which therefore models for us our relationship to one another. The characteristic of God's freedom has been undervalued and needs renewed attention. It is not the easiest aspect of the biblical testimony about God to claim. Because it encompasses the whole of God's word, it is sometimes difficult to describe in a brief and succinct way what we mean by the freedom of God. Basically we are speaking of the way in which the many aspects of God's relationship to us come constantly as freely given gifts, and not as elements we can in any way control or manage. We can only receive and respond to the possibilities of relationship God has given.

In Deuteronomy 7:7-8, God speaks through Moses: "It was not because you were more numerous than any other people that the Lord set his heart on you and chose you. . . . It was because the Lord loved you." We did not obligate God into relationship. It is not out of obligation, but out of freely given grace that God has called us into relationship. Through the modeling of God's freedom in relation to us, we learn to value our own independence and individuality as that which enables us to give ourselves freely in relationship to others. We learn the worth of our humanness in all its richness and variety. We come to value the gift of the humanness we each possess, and have to give to another . . . and another . . . and another in the web of our relationships. We discover that part of our full humanness which can be given only in relationship, and not coerced or controlled.

To understand what is meant by "the freedom of God," we focus here on four different themes from the biblical testimony where we see the freedom of God demonstrated.

1. The first is God's freedom as witnessed in the creation itself. Creation is the freely given gift of God. God was not in some way obligated to create the world, but God did so as an act of freely given divine grace. It is the first act of God's freedom that God resolved to call the world into being. And the world that God called into being was one that included the possibilities of relationship—to God, to one another as human beings, and to the whole of God's creation.

When we ponder that freely given gift of our own createdness, there are, of course, many rich themes that can be pointed to. Here there is room only to sample the rich creation material of the Old Testament, and we do so by looking at elements that illumine our created capacity for relationship.

First of all, in the Hebrew tradition *creation is good.* We are so used to the Genesis 1 creation story with its recurring refrain, "And God saw that it was good," that we take it for granted.

We forget what a revolutionary statement that was in the ancient world of which it was a part. We fail to see how revolutionary that statement could again be if we heard it in a new and fresh way. There are many people living in our own time who do not accept the notion that the creation is good, and we need to claim that message anew.

In Genesis 1:31, at the end of the six days of creation, the account, summing up the whole of that creative work, says, "God saw all that was made, and behold, it was *very* good" (author's trans.). Those were surprising words to many in the ancient world of biblical times. It was not the commonly accepted view that the creation was good. In that ancient time, the world was experienced by many as something like a minefield that had to be renegotiated on a daily basis. In the religions of Egypt, Mesopotamia, and Canaan, the world was thought to be inhabited by divine powers lurking and hovering in all the elements of nature, and therefore liable to be offended or intruded upon at any given moment. These powers were not thought to be benevolent in purpose; in fact, they were considered dangerous. Think how different that is from the Genesis claim that creation is intended by God for good. Think how different it is to live confidently in a world that reiterates that claim—affirming anew in every age that we are intended by God to live in a good world, filled with blessings that we can experience and which lead to our wholeness.

The creation is good, and therefore it is possible for us to claim, even in a broken world, the vision of that goodness as God's plan for creation in the first place. Unlike those of the ancient world, we do not need magic and divination as a central portion of our religious life to protect us from dangerous powers that have no interest in our well-being.

The experience of creation as good was intended by God for all. And in God's creation all are interrelated. The goodness God intended is experienced only in relationship to others, to nature, and to God's own self (see Genesis 2:9, 18, 21-24). When the goodness of creation is broken by acts of sin that deny wholeness and full life to others, all are affected because we are created in relationship. We shall speak further of this interrelatedness in chapter 4.

A second theme from the biblical witness to creation is that we are created in the *image of God*, male and female (Genesis 1:26ff.). For our concerns, this is surely one of the most important of the biblical texts, but once again this text is so familiar that we sometimes take it for granted.

What do we mean by "created in the image of God"? One of the dangerous distortions in the history of the Christian tradition has been the constant tendency to limit that notion of "the image of God" to some one aspect of our humanness. Over the centuries, many elements of our humanity have been singled out as the locus for the image of God—the soul within, the capacity for reason, free will, and so on. These are important parts of our created humanness, but they do not fully express and encompass what this biblical text means by "creation in the image of God." Unlike the Greeks of later Hellenistic times, the Hebrews were very reluctant to subdivide our humanity. They were constantly concerned about reemphasizing our wholeness, in all its many dimensions. Therefore, "creation in the image of God" had less to do with some theoretical aspect of our makeup than it had to do with our function as whole beings in the created world.

"The image of God" has something to do with testimony in this creation story to the purpose for which we were created. It was the custom, in the ancient world, for kings and pharaohs to erect an image of themselves in the far-flung corners of their empires to remind people in that place of who truly reigned there. In the creation story in Genesis 1, a salient emphasis is that of the sovereignty of a divine creator whose very word calls things into being. The picture is one of divine power and majesty. Within that portrait of a divine creator-sovereign who nevertheless intended for us a benevolent, good world, we come to the creation of humanity. God resolves that both male and female should be created in the image of God, suggesting that both men and women are to live in the created world as those who represent God's true reign over all the earth.

Seeking for a way to understand relationship to

that creator God, those who gave us the testimony of the creation story in Genesis 1 are suggesting to us that our created role in the midst of God's whole creation is not to exercise some power of our own, some inherent right to do with the world what we wish for our own narrow human purposes, but to *represent,* to show forth the sovereignty of God. We are to be the trustees of God's ultimate reign, not our own. To be created in the image of God, therefore, is to represent God's ultimate creative sovereignty through our lives and interrelationships in the created order. We point to the One who created and who cares for it all. We are not merely empowered to seek our own narrow interests. Thus, our own relationships to God, to others, and to nature are for the sake of furthering the welfare of God's whole creation, and we can never justifiably limit ourselves to our own self-interest or self-fulfillment apart from those relationships.

This wider responsibility is seen in Genesis 1:28, where those created in the image of God are then given dominion over all the earth and its creatures. Our dominion is now understood as representative of the Creator's dominion; our purpose becomes that of trustees of creation. Our relationships to one another and to nature are to reflect the responsibility that comes with creation in the image of God.

A third aspect of God's freedom seen in creation is the fact that we were created with *free will,* the ability to choose. The commandment

not to eat of the tree of the knowledge of good
and evil in Genesis 2:16-17 means that human
beings are given the capacity by God to choose
obedience or disobedience, wholeness or brokenness. More will be said about this later, but
we need to understand free will from the very
beginning as a divine risk. God freely took the
risk of giving us meaningful choices to make,
and that's what makes relationship possible. By
extension, our relationships are possible to their
fullest only when we take the risk of giving one
another, in the various relationships of which
we are a part, the freedom to make meaningful
choices.

So often, our energies in relationship are
devoted to control and manipulation. These
practices restrict choice and confine choice to
predetermined roles. God's risk in giving us the
possibility for free and meaningful choice was a
terrible risk, because with the free gift of choice
comes the possibility of brokenness as well.
Relationship always involves that risk. We
become vulnerable.

Before we leave creation, we need to look at one
way of viewing creation theology that has greatly
distorted our notion of relationships. It is the
distortion of *hierarchical thinking.* Imagine a
diagonal line, with God at the top and the earth at
the bottom. In this view, the emphasis is always
that God is "spirit" and the character of the earth
is "material." Everything in the created order is
arranged in a hierarchy, with God at the top of the

scale and the earth at the bottom of the scale. The position of various parts of creation along that diagonal line is also taken to indicate the moral worth of each part of creation. The higher up the line the position is, and the closer to God, the greater the moral worth; the lower on the line, and the closer to the material earth, the less the moral worth.

This way of thinking about creation emerged in New Testament times and is reflected in some of the late New Testament texts. It becomes particularly strong during the early centuries of the church and is given new impetus and power in some aspects of Augustine's thinking and teaching. It has reigned almost unchallenged in significant segments of the Western church tradition. We are influenced by this way of thinking even when we are not conscious of it.

The top of the hierarchy is defined in terms of "spirit" and the bottom of the hierarchy is defined in terms of the "material." Immediately we should begin to have suspicions about this way of thinking about things. At the heart of our faith testimony is an incarnation where the Word became flesh and dwelt among us (see John 1:14). What in the world were we thinking of, with an incarnation at the center of our faith, to then allow ourselves to accept uncritically a hierarchical way of thinking about the creation, one that divides the spiritual and the material as if they were the positive and negative poles of our experience? No wonder that issues like those of human sexuality and the physical dimensions of human relationship have been so distorted in the life of the church!

What is more, this hierarchical view included and arranged everything else from high to low along the scale, theoretically going from humans to animals to plants and then to the material earth itself. But in reality, however, already in the first century the Christian hierarchy began to be subdivided arbitrarily. The arrangement went like this: God, males, females, races other than whatever one I belong to, Jews, animals, plants, and the inanimate earth.

The murder of a Jew, in the medieval law codes, was in the same section, and punishable with the same penalty, as poaching the king's deer, because Jews were thought to be little more than animals. They were thought to have tumbled collectively, and for all time, down the hierarchical scale, because of the sin of "deicide."

Racism has been empowered by this hierarchical way of thinking about creation from very early centuries onward through the notion that some races occupy a lower position on the scale of creation. There is a scene in the television epic "Roots" where the granddaughter of Kunta Kinte is being taught how to read by the daughter of the plantation owner. They are discovered, and because it is against the laws of the state of Virginia to teach a black person to read, terrible consequences follow. The granddaughter is sold away from her family into new slaveholding hands. The statute on the Virginia state books in that period of time says that persons of the darkskinned races were not to be taught to read, because reading was a skill reserved to the "higher orders of creation." In the legislation itself, a distorted theological justification based on hierarchical thinking about creation was included in the law code to justify racist practices.

We all know how often the hierarchical elevation of men and the subordination of women have been justified by the notion that women occupy a rung of the creation ladder farther from God and closer to the earth. The stereotypes are all too familiar to us: Women are more "earthy" and "material," and men are supposed to be more "spiritual" and "intellectual." It is not accidental that Protestant churches started ordaining women in significant numbers only within the last several decades, and women are still excluded from ordained ministry in many churches. One of the great foundation stones for excluding women from the ordained ministry is the notion that they are not close enough to God, not spiritual enough. It is said that because of the sin of Eve, they as women have tumbled down the hierarchical scale farther away from God. The biblical creation account does not read in this way, but that has become the tradition in the West.

In short, this distortion of hierarchical understanding of creation has been one of the bases of racism, sexism, and anti-Semitism in the West throughout the entire history of Western Christianity.

What is insidious about this hierarchy is that so many human minorities are harmed by it. The poor are often inserted somewhere on the lower end, as if to be poor is to be farther from God's care. Gay men and lesbian women are also inserted on the lower end, as if sexual orientation automatically places one farther from God. And people of particular life-styles or beliefs are inserted on the lower end, as if by differences of opinion one distances oneself from God's care and concern.

God's free gift in creation is the gift of life in relationship, which seeks the wholeness of the entire creation. As those created in the image of God we both receive and help enable the goodness of creation in our interrelated lives. Each of our relationships is to be understood as a part of God's gift of creation and part of our responsibility within creation.

2. God's freedom is shown to us not only in the creation material, but also in the covenant material. Chapter 3 is devoted in detail to the covenant concept and what it means to talk about covenant in relationship. Here in relation to God's freedom, we simply observe that relationship as God's covenant people is also initiated as God's free gift. In the covenant materials we discover God's free gift in calling us into peoplehood.

Our story as a community of faith begins not in the obligation of God to be related to us as a people, but in God's summons of us into free relationship in covenant community. When our ancestors were slaves in Egypt, God initiated their deliverance (Exodus 1–15) and called them into covenant relationship (19–20) out of freely given divine grace. Our covenant God is a God of radical freedom.

The God of radical freedom, in the very beginning of our story as a covenant people, says through Moses to those people, "I will be merciful to whom I will be merciful" (Exodus 33:19 author's trans.). We do not like this verse because it sounds like divine arbitrariness. It is not! It is divine freedom. The church hasn't liked this verse very well because the church has been distressingly prone to make its own lists of those who are deserving of God's mercy. "Certainly not those people with AIDS over there!" Over and over again, the church thinks it can define those who are deserving of God's mercy and pass that list on to God. And the prophets, and Jesus, and the apostles, and others over the generations, have had to rise up and remind us over and over again that God's grace, and our relationship to God as a covenant people, come as a gift, and that God's story will *always* be larger than our story. Think for example, of all those with whom Jesus associated who were considered by the religious authorities to be outcasts, criminals, unclean persons, or simply sinners, and therefore not worthy of God's grace or the community's care in relationship.

God's people have always had to be reminded of

this. The tendency is always to substitute, for the radical freedom of God, the domestication of God. We desire a God who can be controlled in behalf of those *we* have determined are deserving of God's mercy. We often seek to control where and when and in what form God's mercy is to be experienced.

The radical freedom of God crops up also in Israel's history, struggling with the notion of divine freedom, and always being tempted to domesticate God in behalf of its own interests through idolatry or special interest religion (e.g., see Jeremiah's temple sermon in Jeremiah 7).

Just as relationship to God cannot be controlled but must be received as a gift, so too, our relationships with others are not intended to encompass and control, but, to be meaningful, must preserve the freedom of those who enter into relationship. Relationship to others must come as a gift to be offered and received.

3. Alongside God's freedom in creation and God's freedom in covenant, is God's freedom in *history*. We know our God to be a God of radical freedom. One of the things about radically free gods is that they have a distressing way of popping up in the most surprising places! Here's one instance of biblical testimony to God's radical freedom in history.

In the time of the Babylonian Exile, Israel's depth of despair is expressed in the words of the 137th psalm:

By the rivers of Babylon—
  there we sat down and there we wept
  when we remembered Zion.
On the willows there
  we hung up our harps.
For there our captors
  asked us for songs,
and our tormentors asked for mirth, saying,
  "Sing us one of the songs of Zion!"
How could we sing the Lord's song
  in a foreign land?

Do you hear the implied answer there? The implied answer is, "We can't. Don't ask us, we've already hung up the instruments." And that's what exile is all about. It's not geography. Exile is the time when the songs don't come.

The remarkable thing about that experience of exile is that in the midst of it came one of the most hopeful voices in the entire Scripture. An anonymous prophet whom we call only Second Isaiah or Deutero-Isaiah declared to the non-singers, "Sing to the Lord a new song," and then had the audacity to look in new places for where that song might be found. That prophet, among other things, scanned the horizon looking for the hopeful signs of God's wholeness-making, grace-giving activity and said in effect, "Look, over there on the horizon." "Behold Cyrus, my anointed, he will break down the bars of your captivity. I call him by name, though he knows me not" (Isaiah 45:1ff. paraphrase). Do you know what the people said? The text clearly indicates, in the anger of the prophet following this oracle, that this was not a well-received word. Cyrus was the pagan king of Persia. Imagine thinking of Cyrus as God's anointed. The Hebrew word for anointed is "messiah." What? Cyrus? He didn't go through the membership class! He's definitely not ordained. And the prophet says, "Thus says the Lord . . . 'I have aroused Cyrus in righteousness; . . . he shall build my city and set my exiles free' " (45:11, 13). "I call you by your name . . . though you do not know me" (45:4).

To take seriously what it means to be called into relationship to a radically free God means that some of our energies ought always to be devoted to scanning the horizon looking for the grace-bringing, wholeness-making activity of God and joining it, rather than thinking, once we get things organized, God will be obligated to join us. This is crucially important in our human relationships as well. We cannot do our work in the church, reflecting on the difficult moral issues of human relationship including our sexuality, without looking for the operation of God's grace in the insights of the natural sciences and the social sciences, and all of those other areas of human society struggling with these same issues. We will find there alliances that may not fit easily into budget years, and quadrennial emphases and Lenten themes. We will find there insights that may not fit easily into established doctrine and belief. God is a radically free God, sovereign in all of history. If we think we can look for the activity of that God related to any issue by using our institutional resources alone, we simply have too narrow a God and have not taken God's freedom seriously.

4. Finally, God's freedom is manifest in redemption. We see this especially in the life, death, and resurrection of Jesus Christ. Jesus is well aware of that notion of the freedom of God. In fact, it is one of the messages he has difficulty getting across to the disciples. Do you remember that parable of the workers where some came early and some came late, but they were all paid the same wages (Matthew 20:1-16)? Those who came early were distressed by this. It didn't seem fair. But Jesus' point is that we cannot begrudge God's mercy freely given to whomever God wills. Why? Because once again we are dealing with the freedom of God. It is a difficult parable to hear because there is something that offends us. We are right there with the earlycomers protesting the unfairness. Our problem with this parable is that most of us good church people think we are among the earlycomers. But originally, that parable probably had to do with the Jews and the Gentiles. The Jews were the earlycomers and the Gentiles were the latecomers. Most of us are descendants of the latecomers!

Paul talks about the freedom of God. He goes right back to that text, "I will be merciful to whom I will be merciful," and quotes it in Romans 9:15 to remind us that relationship in faith comes as a gift. It does not come by the obligations we lay on God. Likewise, relationship to one another comes as a gift, and not by the obligations we lay on one another.

Radically free gods are not easy to live with, given our natural tendency to seek control. We are tempted to domesticated gods. We are tempted to gods that are somehow manageable. And so, too, relationship as free persons to one another is difficult for those whose desire is to control or manage those relationships and to limit the risk we take in relationship. We are tempted to domesticate relationships by defining them through rigid roles, and customs, and laws that minimize the risk of freedom. We are tempted to manage those relationships rather than receive them as gifts and respond to them in our own freedom. It is so much easier to let defined patterns rule, but from God we learn of the freedom that esteems our own integrity and worth and makes true relationship possible. From God we also learn that the freedom *from*, out of which comes our individuality and independence, must also become freedom *for*. Freedom *from* the other becomes, in God's story, freedom *for* the other. Alongside freedom, with its stress on individuality and independence, must be laid the qualities of freedom for the other, with its themes of vulnerability and interdependence. It is to those themes that we turn next.

CHAPTER 2

Relationship as Vulnerability

*A*s important and central as freedom is in our own relationships, and as important and central as the freedom of God is in our understanding of relationship to God, that quality of character is not enough for a full understanding of what relationship means—either relationship to God or relationship to one another in human community. Freedom left alone can become remoteness, arrogance, aloofness. What is significant about our faith story is that a radically free God chose to become engaged and involved in our experience, and to do so at the point of our deepest woundedness and need. So we must move from speaking about freedom to speaking of other things that must accompany that quality of freedom.

As a boy, I was particularly fascinated with Superman. That wasn't really unusual in the time in which I grew up. It was typical of many boys to be enthralled with Superman. All those comic books, movies, and television shows were very popular, and I was hooked! I knew everything about Superman. I knew he was from Krypton, and, of course, I knew that he was faster than a speeding bullet, more powerful than a locomotive, and able to leap tall buildings in a single bound. But the quality I liked best about Superman was his *invulnerability*. (To tell you the truth, I think I also liked knowing such an impressive word.) But it was there in the comic books. Superman was *invulnerable*. Bullets bounced off his chest. Crowbars bent around his head. I wished that I were invulnerable.

Now the opposite of invulnerability is *vulnerability*. To be vulnerable is defined as "able to be wounded." Someone who is invulnerable is someone who cannot be wounded. I believe that Superman became for many growing up in my time a model or a reflection of how we were taught to be. It is considered desirable—for little boys it is even considered manly—to render ourselves incapable of being wounded. At least, we were supposed to act as if we could not be wounded. Thus it is not uncommon to encounter men or women who seem to have modeled their lives after the Rock of Gibraltar. I have come to believe, deeply and fervently, that the life-style of the Rock of Gibraltar is more appropriate to insurance companies than to human beings.

Many churches in their style of community and many individuals in their patterns of family, friendship, and sexuality have adopted "Superman" styles of relationship, faith, and ministry. We are all trying to be Supermen and Superwomen—to relate without risking woundedness.

It affects our lives as congregations. It affects our lives as individuals. It affects our lives as relational and sexual beings.

Churches with the Superman and Superwoman life-style tend to devise their programs in ways that avoid risks, or at least greatly minimize them. Success is the frequent watchword. We seek efficient and effective programs with results we can see and measure. Thus we plan only for goals that fit our budget years, and our Lenten emphases, and our committee structures, and our quadrennial concerns.

We take few risks, but many of the goals to which the church is genuinely called do not fit well into such patterns. They require risk. They require not Superman and Superwoman categories, but congregations willing to risk their own woundedness for the sake of the world's wounds. Think of some of the tasks to which we are called, and imagine that we could pursue them without risking our own woundedness: seeking peace in a nuclear age; feeding the hungry in a limited world; bringing hope and focus to families fragmented by social pressures; fostering community in a day still plagued by economic and racial divisions; nourishing the spirit in an age of materialism; recovering the wholeness of our human sexuality in an age that exploits sexual imagery. These are long-term tasks that the church cannot pursue if its image of itself is invulnerability, success, and minimal risk. These are the long-term tasks that require long-term commitment, which continues working even when the results are few and the risk is great. They will never fit patterns of "management by objective," or goals designed for short-term gain. These tasks are the visionary tasks that have always caused the world to label us as foolish.

Many of us as individuals also are tempted by Superman and Superwoman styles and outlooks. We think that persons of faith are to be positive, efficient, creative, and success-oriented. That's the kind of people we want in our churches and our lives. We don't want people who bring problems with them. We often kid ourselves that being faithful means only being positive and happy. Have you ever run into one of those people who say, "I've found Jesus, and now I'm happy, happy, happy!" When I run into one of those people, I think, What is going to happen to this person when life deals them and their happiness a blow? Do they have a faith able to provide resources for them in the midst of that? Why hasn't someone told them that faith has something to say to those deep recesses where they feel their own wounds. Finding Jesus has something to do with being wounded, not just being happy, happy, happy! It has to do with recognizing our own wounds in the wounds of Jesus, and in this recognition finding our mission to minister to the wounds of the world.

Many who need the church most are not on top of it all. They are in need. Many of the times we most need the church and the resources of our faith are the times we experience uncertainty, doubt, grief, pain, and failure. Where in the church's life and our relationships as people of faith do we encourage the sharing of our need? Where can we take the risk of admitting those needs, admitting that we are not invulnerable, and that faith does not make us invulnerable? Where does the church really risk sharing the world's needs and the world's wounds? If we can't even acknowledge our own wounds, can we ever acknowledge and face the world's wounds?

Many in our culture are urged as sexual beings to Superman and Superwoman styles and attitudes. We are bombarded with media images and commercial products that promote sexual performance over the wholeness of our sexuality. We are bombarded with media images and commercial products that elevate *image* over relationship as the basis for our sexuality. We are made to feel inadequate if our sex isn't super sex. We are made to feel as if sexuality is something we master, rather than receive as a gift.

We are producing a generation of people plagued by manipulative and shallow views of sexuality, destroying the possibility of deep and intimate relationships.

We are producing a generation of people in which sexual abuse has reached all-time highs.

We are producing a generation of people where patterns of sexual addiction cripple men and women and codependence destroys their families.

But the church is largely silent. We are producing a generation of sexually wounded people waiting for a word from the church—waiting for a time when these struggles are not the hidden struggles; where discussions are not relegated to the margins of a church's life or avoided in the name of avoiding conflict. These are central concerns in our society and in people's personal lives. Why have they remained marginal or controversial concerns to the church's life?

Once again, we must turn to the image of God out of which we understand all matters of relationship. One of the problems contributing to the silence of the churches is a problem of our portrait of God. We are accustomed to thinking of God in categories such as: omnipotent, invincible, mighty, majestic, sovereign, immutable. It is not that these qualities are absent from the biblical story. What is really crucial about the portrait of God in our biblical story is that these qualities are not there alone. It is not the power of our God that represents a unique claim in the ancient world. Egypt, Mesopotamia, Canaan—in the religion of every society in the ancient world it was claimed that the gods were powerful. What is different about the claim of our biblical story is that a God possessed of power chose to become vulnerable, wounded. It is the side of God's character we have neglected, much to our peril. It is the quality of God to be spoken of here as the *vulnerability* of God. It is not the side of God we normally sing of in our hymns, but it is out of this side of the divine character that intimacy and relationship grow.

In chapter 1 we talked about Genesis 1. We talked about the portrait of God's sovereignty; the power of a creator God whose very Word calls the world into being, whose divine resolve creates us in the image of God, male and female, and calls us to the task of representing that image in the midst of creation. We need to couple with that picture of creative sovereignty, the picture of creative intimacy that follows in Genesis 2:4*b*-9. For in that testimony to our creation faith, we find the portrait of a God who takes up the very dust of the earth. Like a loving craftsperson, God fashions the *'adam* (humanity) from the *'adamah* (soil). The soil and the human creature—in Hebrew these words are related. A loving artisan God takes up the earth and fashions an "earth creature."[1]

The intimacy of relationship between God and human and earth is eloquently presented in this story. What could be more intimate than God breathing the divine breath into the nostrils of the earth creature in order to give humanity animation and life? "'*adam* became a living being" (Genesis 2:7). It is a picture of the intimacy of God (Genesis 2) alongside the portrait of the sovereignty of God (Genesis 1). It is the juxtaposition of these aspects of God's character that is remarkable and unique about our faith tradition and our faith story.

The portrait of God in Genesis 2 is the portrait

of a God who risks relationship. Did you ever think of this creation story as the first story of the woundedness of God? Is there an experience of woundedness any more painful than to come searching for one you love, and find that your loved one has hidden from you (Genesis 3:8ff.)?

The vulnerability of God is a quality we have often neglected in our desire to identify with the power and majesty of God. Identifying with the power and majesty of God makes us feel powerful. James Wharton has defined vulnerability as "choosing to be so intimately involved in the story of another that what happens in their life, for good or for ill, becomes part of our own story."[2] This is what God has done. God has chosen to make the human story a part of the divine story as well. God is indeed powerful and sovereign, but God has chosen to become involved in a passionate sharing and caring relationship to all humanity. And God has done that at the point of our deepest need, our deepest pains, our deepest woundedness.

One of the most important texts in the entire scripture is the seventh verse of Exodus 3. It is a part of the story of Moses' encounter with God at the burning bush. The bush served to get Moses' attention so that he could then hear the important word of God. For us too, the bush is to be just the attention getter we need in order to hear a very important divine word. What God said to Moses out of the burning bush was, "I have seen the affliction of my people who are in Egypt. I have heard their cry because of their taskmasters. I know their sufferings, and I have come down to deliver them" (Exodus 3:7 author's trans.).

For a basic, foundational understanding of the biblical witness to God's character, one can hardly do better than to begin with the four verbs in this verse: a God who sees, hears, knows, and delivers. A God who sees and hears is already testimony to a God who is not content to be aloof and remote, but who *cares* about the pain and the outcry of people. In Exodus 2:23-24 we read, "The Israelites groaned under their slavery, and cried out. . . . God heard their groaning." It doesn't say, "The people prayed." They just cried out in pain, and God heard. They didn't have to couch their cries in some acceptable, pious manner. Following God's example, we have to find more places in the life of the church where we simply hear outcries for what they are; we have to find more places where we see, hear, and care.

The most remarkable verb in this verse is the third one. God says, "I know their sufferings." The verb "to know" in Hebrew is not as limited in its range and meaning as our English word for "know." We usually think of knowing as cognitive knowledge, book knowledge. In Hebrew, *yada'* means "to enter into and experience that which is known; to participate in that which is known." It is a word that bespeaks the definition of vulnerability James Wharton gives us. It is a word that captures the notion of making another's story one's own story. So when God says,

"I know your sufferings," it is one of the most remarkable and revolutionary statements in the entire ancient world. The divine voice says in effect, "I participate in your sufferings. I experience your sufferings." Further, God says this to a group of slaves in Egypt, a people absolutely insignificant by the world's standards, the dispossessed.

That was not what gods and goddesses were known to be in the ancient world! Gods and goddesses in the ancient world were identified with the power centers. If the pharaoh was powerful, it was said that the pharaoh's gods were powerful. And if the pharaoh was defeated in battle, it would be said that someone else's gods were more powerful on that day. To look for divine presence in the ancient world was to look for the power centers. Imagine how startling it was for a God, our God, to say, "I know their sufferings. I participate in their sufferings. I experience their sufferings."

This is the beginning of a continuing tradition of our God as a God who suffers with our sufferings, who is wounded with our woundedness. This testimony to a suffering God continues on through the Old Testament witness to God as one who is especially involved in and concerned for the lives of those in pain, need, and suffering even when they believe they have been forgotten.

> But Zion said, "The Lord has forsaken me,
> my Lord has forgotten me."

Can a woman forget her nursing child,
    or show no compassion for the child of
    her womb?
Even these may forget,
    yet I will not forget you.
                        (Isaiah 49:14-15)

This theme finds for us its fullest and deepest expression in the testimony to Jesus Christ as God incarnate in our midst, suffering death on the cross, fully experiencing human suffering and pain, fully wounded with our woundedness for the sake of a wounded world. The cross represents not God's glorification of suffering, but God's participation in our suffering and death. God knows the depths of our experience but in the Resurrection declares that wholeness and life have a further word of hope and possibility to make visible in the world through God's grace.

It is significant, given the focus of this study, that we recognize that the verb "to know" is one of the central verbs used in the Bible to describe human relationship. Modeled on God's knowing of us, "to know" is the verb used to encompass human relationship *including* our sexuality. It is the very same verb that appears in genealogies. "X *knew* his wife X, and she conceived and gave birth to a child, X." It suggests that entering into and experiencing another's story is at the heart of human relationship, and that this clearly and consciously includes the sexual dimension of that relationship. It is a word meant to characterize *both* our personal and our social relationships. Further, to know (experience) others in relationship is to be, following God's example, especially concerned about bearing one another's burdens— sharing the pain and suffering of others' lives and of a broken world. It is to become vulnerable.

It is this very word "to know" which Jeremiah employs when he speaks to those who have once again tried to claim the reality of God for the powerful (Jeremiah 22:15-16 italics added):

> Are you a king
>   because you compete in cedar?
> Did not your father eat and drink
>   and do justice and righteousness?
>   Then it was well *[shalom]* with him.
> He judged the cause of the poor and needy;
>   then it was well *[shalom]*.
> Is not this to *know* me?
>   says the Lord.

Although there is much more that could be said about the theme of the vulnerability of God, we have room here only to point up briefly two additional images, one from the Old Testament and one from the New Testament, which reflect the vulnerability of God and model for us something of our vulnerability to one another in relationship.

The Old Testament makes frequent reference to God's compassion. It is one of the qualities mentioned most often about God and God's relationship to us. Our God is a God of compassion. We have not explored this image very deeply. Our tendency is to confuse compassion with sympathy or pity. It is much more than sympathy or pity. The Hebrew word from which compassion comes is *rehem*, which in the singular means "womb" or "uterus." In the plural, it is used to denote a quality of God's care for us, and therefore a quality of our care for one another. In the plural, this word is translated "compassion" or "love."

Phyllis Trible suggests that what *rehem* really means when it is translated "compassion" is "womb love."[3] It points to the complete interrelationship of two lives, as in a mother carrying a child. Thus God's compassion is a metaphor born of the womb, and it speaks to us of God's total involvement with the people of God. It is an image of God with us—a remarkable image of life participating in life, individual and yet united. What image could better express what God's compassion and our own compassion toward one another should be like? Listen to these remarkable passages where God speaks to Israel in such images:

> Hearken to me, O house of Jacob . . .
> who have been borne by me from your birth,
>   carried by me from the womb;
> even to your old age, I am here,
>   and to gray hairs, I will carry you.
> I have conceived you, and I have borne you;
>   I have carried you, and I will save you.
>   (Isaiah 46:3-4 author's trans.)

Can a woman forget her nursing child,
   or show no compassion for the child of her
      womb?
Even these may forget,
   yet I will not forget you.
                         (Isaiah 49:15)

Is Ephraim my dear Son?
   Is he my darling child?
The more I speak of him,
   the more I do remember him.
Therefore my womb trembles for him;
   I will truly show compassion upon him,
      says the Lord.
             (Jeremiah 31:20 author's trans.)

These are remarkable images of an aspect of God we have almost completely neglected in the life of the church. The concept of God's compassion is a metaphor born of the womb, telling us of the total involvement in the lives and stories of one another, which is the very essence of the community to which we are called as the people of God. God has already demonstrated that community with us. In our relationships we are to be intimately and vulnerably related to one another in the way that God's compassionate involvement with us has modeled.

Let us turn to a New Testament image, taken from a story about Jesus in Luke 8:43-48. A woman ill for twelve years with a flow of blood manages to make her way through a great crowd surrounding

Jesus, and with great effort, touches the hem of his garment. She is immediately healed. It is a remarkable story, a remarkable testimony to the faith and perseverance of a woman wounded and suffering who imagined that the step toward healing might involve touching and dared to risk that touch. This is remarkable in itself. And her healing, of course, is a great miracle.

Equally remarkable is another aspect of the story that is often neglected. It is the fact that in the midst of a great, jostling throng of people, Jesus immediately says, "Who touched me?" Not only is Jesus surrounded by a throng, he is urgently on his way to minister to the dying daughter of a great ruler of the synagogue. He has an important task to accomplish, one that may give him influence with the powerful decision makers of his society. But when someone in need of healing reaches out to touch him, he instantly knows and responds. In Jesus Christ, we see God's sensitivity to our need for healing, love, and wholeness, and God's willingness to be touched by that need. In the woman, we see one whose faith sought wholeness in the risk of touching another.

When we so often wonder why our church, our denomination, our congregations, our own personal lives, our ministries as the people of God do not touch more lives, can it possibly be that we are too unwilling to *be* touched? or to recognize the touch of those seeking healing, love, and wholeness? Surely touching, and being touched, is at the heart of what it means to be the bearers of Good News! If we are to speak to the woundedness of relationships in our generation, as those in the church who respond to the needs of the wounded, then we have something to teach the church and the wider community about touching and being touched in all the aspects of our lives and ministries. Touching and being touched become signs of our willingness to become vulnerable to one another and thereby to risk the possibilities of fulfilling and renewing relationship.

When we know the vulnerability of God, we become a different kind of community. We become the community of the Psalms, that remarkable collection of materials drawn out of the worship life of Israel which can encompass both the laments and the thanksgivings. In remarkably candid terms, the Psalms can take the deepest wounds and offer them up to God, transforming woundedness into thanksgiving, not by sweeping those wounds under the rug but by acknowledging them before God. "My God, my God, why have you forsaken me?" opens the twenty-second psalm (the verse used in Jesus' cry of dereliction from the cross). The Psalms honestly express our deepest wounds. But that kind of honesty about woundedness is not the end of the story, for Psalm 22 goes on to express some of the most eloquent lines of praise in the entire psalter (vv. 23-31). There we see the community capable

of encompassing both woundedness and thanksgiving, not as we so often imagine, where the one
drives out the other. Thus too, the cry of despair
from the cross becomes the cry of joy at the empty
tomb.

The issues of woundedness with which we deal
are often not issues with which the church wants
to be faced. We cannot allow them to be unvoiced
or to be placed in the sanctity only of the pastor's
study, or hidden from the view of the entire
congregation, which must be mobilized to minister to one another. As Christians we cannot avoid
in our personal relationships the sharing of our
deepest wounds and pains. We must be called to
that different kind of community which grows out
of acknowledging the vulnerability of God—to the
community of the Psalms, from which nothing
central to life in both its wholeness and its
brokenness is absent, or to the community of those
who gather around the Lord's table, where brokenness and wholeness stand side by side, and we
are united at God's table in all our diversity. To
know the vulnerability of God is to suggest an
appropriate image for dealing with the issues of
human relationship that the church so often finds
difficult to face and with the struggles that we fear
to embrace.

One final biblical image comes from the story of
Jacob in Genesis 32. Jacob had lived a self-centered
life, which led him into alienation from his
brother. Having cheated Esau out of his birthright
and blessing, Jacob fled from his brother in fear

of his life, lived and prospered in exile, but finally
came to that moment when, beyond his self-
centeredness, he recognized that he was not whole.
As long as he remained alienated from his brother
he was wounded and lacking in wholeness. Jacob
finally took the risk of a journey, a journey that led
through that dark night on the banks of the Jabbok
River where Genesis 32:24 tells us, "A man
wrestled with him until daybreak." But as the
wrestling continued, Jacob finally recognized that
in this struggle in human form, God was present.
The visitor touched his thigh and it was thrown
painfully out of joint. Jacob, always the controller
and the manipulator, demanded to know the
visitor's name. He received no reply; instead, the
visitor gave him a new name. He was no longer
Jacob, the one of self-interest and manipulation,
but Israel, a name that points toward community.
When the dawn came, Jacob limped from the site
of the struggle, genuinely wounded. And he called
that place "Peniel," which means "face of God."
But the story doesn't end there, for on that very
morning he limped from Peniel to anxiously meet
his brother Esau, not knowing what he would find.
For all he knew, Esau was still resolved to kill him.
He limped anxiously toward that moment of new
meeting, only to find Esau throwing open his arms
in embrace, and pulling him to his breast. Esau
had long since forgiven him. With tears of joy
streaming down his face, Jacob said, "Truly to see
your face is like seeing the face of God" (Genesis 33:10).

If we take seriously the theme of vulnerability as testimony to God's relationship to us and our relationship to one another, and we seek to be vulnerable to the woundedness of persons and communities, then we need to know that the path to full relationships and the journey to wholeness and reconciliation with alienated brothers and sisters will pass through those dark nights where struggles in human form seize us, where we wrestle through what seem like dark nights in the life of the church and in our own personal lives. We will be tempted once again, as we always are, to try to control that struggle. But in our willingness to embrace such struggles as persons and communities of faith, we will find the name promised to us that points toward community. And in our wounds taken from that struggle, we will be enabled to see the face of God in the face of our wounded brothers and sisters. Our God is a God who knows our sufferings and calls us to vulnerability to one another in the risk of relationship.

CHAPTER 3

Relationship as Fidelity

*F*reedom and vulnerability are important qualities of relationship, especially in the area of our sexuality, but left alone, these can become manipulative or capricious. In relationship, they must be coupled with commitment. Hence, we must speak about relationship as fidelity.

Scripture tells us, "For [God's] steadfast love endures forever" (Psalm 136 throughout). Our relationship to God is marked by divine fidelity as well as by divine freedom and vulnerability. Relationship to God, God's steadfast love, is trustworthy. It can be counted upon. God's fidelity is expressed in righteousness and embodied in covenant relationship.

> Steadfast love and faithfulness will meet;
>   righteousness and peace will kiss each other.
>   (Psalm 85:10)

In our own relationships, however, both these terms, righteousness and covenant, are misunderstood and narrowly applied. We need to recover their meaning more fully if we are to understand fidelity in human relationships. We need to ask what it means for our relationships to be marked by commitment and trustworthiness, as well as by freedom and vulnerability.

We too often rigidify concepts of righteousness, fidelity, and covenant in a manner that is more characteristic of the Pharisees' legalism than of the covenant understandings of Moses' time, or the teachings of Jesus. We tend to reduce righteousness, and therefore to reduce covenant relationship, to a rule ethic, in which relationship and righteousness within relationship are fulfilled by mere obedience to the rules that govern relationships through custom, habit, or law. We sometimes spend more time and energy trying to define and teach rules that make decisions for us, than in defining and teaching the values and qualities that we hope will characterize our relationships as full persons.

We cannot simply reduce Christian ethics to what can be called the "ethics of doing," where the central question is, What shall we do about X? (e.g., What do we do about the many challenges and issues that face us concerning human sexuality?). Alongside the "ethics of doing," Christian ethics has also to do with "the ethics of being," the shaping of character, identity, values, and perspectives. Here the central question becomes not only, What shall we do? but also, Who shall we be?

The Bible seldom answers the "doing" question for us, although there are resources there to aid in the decision-making process. We face moral issues the biblical communities could not have imagined, and even those issues which are similar must be decided in radically different settings and circumstances.

The Bible is, however, a central resource in shaping our identity, our being, our character— the values and perspectives we use when we must make decisions. The biblical stories, admonitions, songs, visions, and letters all shape us as persons and communities of faith through our encounter with the biblical witness in the church's preaching, teaching, and liturgy. In this encounter, each generation of the church newly becomes a biblical people.

These are not "either-or" aspects of the life of the church. Our conduct (doing) and our character (being) are both vital elements of the Christian life. They are two dimensions of the church's life equal in importance. We sometimes separate them as if there were interest groups within the life of the church. Bible reading over here (being), and social action over there (doing), and rarely do the two meet. We treat the church like a cafeteria line, where everybody passes through and takes only the foods he or she likes. But being and doing, character and conduct, go together and cannot be separated.

Those who focus on identity alone, without any concern for how that is lived out in decision making, run the risk of becoming the "fossil church," locked in the past as an end in itself (e.g., Bible-reading groups that never see beyond the walls of the room where they meet). You know what a fossil is—an extraordinarily faithful witness to the past, but incapable of being anything new and different for the future. On the other hand, those who are so concerned about *doing* something about x or y or z that they leave behind any sense of identity or rootedness in a historical tradition run the risk of becoming the "chameleon church." The chameleon church, having no identity of its own, is prone to take on the coloration of whatever movement, or ideology, or fad, or culture, or perspective happens to surround it. The Christian moral life is lived in the constant tension between being and doing, identity and action.

Thus, to reflect God's righteousness in our relationships to one another is not just a matter of learning the right things to do or rules about when to do them. Righteousness has to do with the quality of our relationships—the identity we carry with us into relationship and the new identity that becomes ours in relationship.

When we think of what it means for our relationships to be characterized by righteousness, we often think of Pharisaic rules, and righteousness is a word we would rather not introduce into the conversation. We think of righteousness as legalistic and self-centered. One of the interesting things about the biblical material is that any careful reading of the biblical understanding of righteousness will tell us that in biblical terms, righteousness was *never* the mere obeying of rules. When those like the Pharisees wished to make it so, Jesus and the prophets before him opposed that narrow understanding of righteousness.

Righteousness is one of the most profound relational terms in the entire Bible. Righteousness always implies the seeking of wholeness in the relationships of which we are a part, whether that is relationship to other individuals or is the larger relationship to society and community. Righteousness is that which seeks to elevate concern for the wholeness of all those others to whom we are related as of equal importance alongside our own wholeness. ("Love your neighbor as yourself.") Indeed, righteousness points to that concept of *inter*relatedness which implies that if *any* are denied wholeness, *we* are less than whole ourselves, because we are interrelated, one to another. Righteousness is what demands of us in each relationship in our lives that we ask, What will fulfill and make this relationship whole? It demands commitment to relationship, not to self.

In fact, the Bible relentlessly resists and opposes the reduction of righteousness to a rule ethic, as if rules could do the job of relating to one another for us. They cannot. When the rules become destructive of relationships, then righteousness *demands* that other options be sought.

A remarkable story in this regard is the story of Tamar (Genesis 38). You will not hear many sermons preached on this text. Tamar is married to one of the sons of Judah. Her husband dies, and one of the customs of that time, to keep people from being left alone and without connectedness to a family and a community, was the practice of Levirate marriage. By this custom Tamar was married to a brother of her husband, one of the other sons of Judah, and he also died. Judah, rather than again provide for her in the family, simply refused to do anything to marry her to another of his sons, or to attach her to a family community. Tamar was left alone, with concerns not only for her own welfare, but also for the welfare of the households of her previous husbands, which, with no marital partner, became her immediate responsibility. She was left with responsibility, but without connectedness to the wider resources and family of her community.

There came a day when Tamar dressed herself as a prostitute and waited at the crossroads until Judah came by. Judah went in to her and had intercourse with her. He gave her a signet, a cord, and a staff to keep as a pledge until he could send back a payment. So he sent back a kid from his flock, but Tamar was gone, and so were Judah's pledges. A short time later, Tamar was discovered to be pregnant, and in the harsh rules of that society, she was judged guilty of the capital offense of adultery and taken out to be burned as a penalty for the offense. She took the signet, the cord, and the staff and sent them to Judah, saying, "It was the owner of these who made me pregnant" (38:25). Judah realized what had happened. Whereas he had refused to provide for the continuity of Tamar's household, Tamar had provided for it herself by her own initiative, and at the risk of her own life. And Judah's response is very interesting. He says, "This woman is more *righteous* than I" (38:26 author's trans.). Although she had violated a rule that called for capital punishment, she had fulfilled the demands of righteousness by seeking wholeness and continuity in the areas of her responsibilities and relationships in the best way she could, at her own initiative, and at risk to her own person.

There are many elements to this story. This ancient story takes place in a strange world and a strange social environment. We do not live in that world. The world in which we must decide, the world in which we must seek wholeness, is very different from the world of Tamar. But this story teaches us that righteousness is never measured simply by the rules as an end in themselves. Righteousness has something to do with our ultimate commitment to that which makes whole the relationships of which we are a part. There are thousands of marriages in all of our communities that fulfill the rules, but they are dehumanizing relationships having little to do with wholeness and are therefore not at their core righteous in the biblical sense. The same might be true of parent-child relationships, friendships, relationships in community or congregation, and relationships in the workplace.

Righteousness is lived out in the context of covenant relationship. Covenant is one of those biblical themes about which we could write an entire book. It is difficult to speak briefly about covenant, because it is such a deep and rich concept in the biblical material. But covenant is so pervasive in the biblical material because it is regarded as so centrally important. The notion of interrelatedness, characterized by commitment to a righteousness that seeks the wholeness of the other, becomes important in all kinds of relationships in the life of the community of faith.

We have explored the concept of covenant more fully for its social and ecclesiastical implications than we have for its application to personal relationships. Yet, we use the language of covenant when we talk about marriage. The term "covenant" frequently appears in the ceremonies and the words we speak, but this often seems an unexplored, unexamined use of the language. We have not looked very deeply into what it might mean to apply the concept of covenant to personal, committed relationships.

Covenant is used in the Scripture to speak of those relationships. It is used to speak of marriage. It is used to speak of deeply committed friendships, such as that of Jonathan and David. It is used to speak of family relationships. Recognizing that covenant is a much larger topic that we cannot fully explore, we will here briefly discuss some misconceptions of covenant applied to the marital relationship where we, as a church, have said that we are to find some of our deepest experiences of committed relationship. Although

marriage is used here for illustration, many of the
observations apply to committed relationships in
general.

The meaning of covenant is widely misunderstood when it is used of marriage. Three misconceptions of covenant need to be clarified in
order to better understand what covenant is. To
do so we must refer back to the language of
covenant in the biblical picture of God's relationship to Israel, and the church's relationship to
God through Christ.

First of all, we should be reminded that
covenant is not security, but trust. Many marry
seeking security, seeking a haven from life's
decisions and uncertainties, but it never succeeds. If we settle for security as the meaning of
covenant, in marriage, or in deeply committed
relationships, then we have settled for less than
what covenant calls for because trust is a much
wider concept than mere security. If anything,
marriage *multiplies* our decisions and responsibilities, and thus, it may increase our anxieties
and insecurities. Relationship to another gives us
responsibility for that life to which we are related,
as well as responsibility for our own life. To
define committed relationship in marriage as
"security" is a self-centered response.

Israel's covenant led it into many strange paths
in relationship to God, and those paths were often
filled with insecurity. For example, deliverance
out of Egypt was not deliverance into the
promised land, but into the wilderness. They

often wished instead for security, and sometimes they tried to grasp for that security. While Moses was on the mountain, they built a golden calf, something solid and secure right where they could control it.

What covenant called for instead was *trust*, which involves the commitment that enables us to avoid tying up all the loose ends in relation to another. Covenant calls for trust in one another, even as we are called to trust in God. This is sometimes difficult when complex lives make us feel insecure and we want to nail things down, when we want patterns that are fixed and stable and secure. How tempting it is to turn to some fixed way we think things should be done and build our own golden calf, which we can control or *think* we can: our way of budgeting, our way of sharing household chores, our way of ordering career priorities, our patterns of sexual relationship. We want something fixed, secure, stable, which usually means we want something we can control.

But covenant calls us to trust in relationship; to live together with the confidence of our support of one another in the midst of complex lives with their insecurities. Covenant is trust that love is stronger than the need for security. It is trust that we can be vulnerable and lower the barriers to one another without fear. Covenant is trust that it is precisely in relationship that we can reveal that all the loose ends are not tied up. And the trust which exists in relationship allows us to accept and risk our own vulnerability, rather than seek always after our security.

Second, *covenant is not bondage, but freedom.* Covenant relationship to another in marriage, or committed partnership, is not bondage, but freedom. It's interesting what the popular language says. Many speak lightly of marriage as giving up your freedom. "Well, I see you're about to lose your freedom." But it is not true.

The language of covenant sometimes sounds like the language of bondage. We speak of the "bonds" of marriage. The exchange of rings is called the "symbol of the binding of one to another." But bondage has to do with the imposition of one will upon another. Israel knew bondage in Egypt, but that was slavery imposed by a strong tyrant. Israel's covenant with God was not bondage, but a relationship voluntarily entered in order to experience the fullness that is possible only in relationship.

Marriage is not the giving up of freedom, but the ultimate use of one's freedom in relationship to another; the freedom to give oneself fully in partnership, in relationship. In marriage, our possibilities are not diminished, but expanded. In relationship, we become more than we could ever be alone. Those who hold themselves apart from relationships of all sorts are not free. They are in bondage to themselves.

In an age that so often stresses self-fulfillment and self-expression and self-awareness, perhaps we need to affirm once again the conviction of our faith that true fulfillment of life is found in relationship to God and to others. Whoever would save his or her life must lose it. The church has something else to say to a world that makes bestsellers of books entitled "Looking Out For Number One." Marriage is, and should be, an expression of a most serious commitment to giving one's life in relationship to another, not in bondage, but in a use of freedom that expands the horizons of one's own personhood. The oneness to be found there, if the relationship is one of mutuality and trust, is a freedom to be persons we could never be apart from each other. It is only as we relate to each other that our freedom to be all that we can be expands.

Finally, a third distortion of covenant: *Covenant is not fixity, but growth.* We have done so little in the church with the theology of marriage and committed relationship. It is not that there are not good materials available, but that these materials are not often available or discussed in local congregations. And curiously, the volumes that appear on the bookstands, with *their* formulas for marriage fulfillment and life fulfillment purely in psycho-social terms, become bestsellers. Why have *we* been so timid about contributing to the vision of what makes for fulfilling, committed relationships? Why have we been so unwilling that the church openly face the difficult issues of relationship? The scandal is not that issues such as those related to human sexuality become controversial in the churches but that many are opposed to taking up these issues at all.

This attitude in the church extends to our personal relationship where we want fixed understandings rather than the uncertainty of growth toward new understandings together.

Covenant is not fixity, but growth. What happens in the marriage ceremony does not establish a marriage relationship for all time, and what is really curious is that so many who marry have not been told that. It merely plants a seed of commitment from which relationship can grow.

Israel's covenant was not static. It had to change and adapt itself to new situations, but always with faith and trust in relationship to God. So, too, we must grow and change, but in relationship to each other. There is a great temptation, at some point in marriage, and in other relationships, to fix things. To set them in concrete. We come to points where we have grown fairly comfortable in the way things are, and we say as Israel did in the wilderness, "Hey, Moses! Why don't we camp at this oasis? It's comfortable here. Did the pillar of cloud and fire move out? I don't want to hear about it!" We think all is going well. Why can't it just go on like this? Then, after we thought we had fixed things in concrete, we wake up years later suddenly to find that the growth needed to meet the new changes in a new time in our life has not taken place, and we are in a dying relationship, rather than a growing relationship.

I happen to live in Maryland. Maryland is famous for the crabs taken out of Chesapeake Bay and shipped all around the country. The life cycle of that crab can teach us an interesting lesson. In order to grow, a crab must, from time to time, shed its shell, and grow a newer and bigger one. When this happens, a crab is extremely vulnerable until the new shell hardens. So each stage of growth requires a risk on the part of the crab, a vulnerability. Each shell becomes a little more rigid. Better protection. Tougher. Harder. Through each succeeding stage, the crab builds its armor. Each stage lasts longer, and the times of vulnerability and risk grow farther apart, until finally the crab succeeds in creating the "ultimate shell," a shell so tough that it will protect from all enemies. But there comes a day when the crab discovers that it has a shell so tough that it cannot be shed. Growth is no longer possible, and that becomes the shell in which the crab dies.

So it is with our relationships, and especially with a marriage. We must grow in relationship, and that means change from comfortable patterns, which will require risk. We risk making ourselves vulnerable to each other for the sake of growth, understanding that true relationship can never be fixed at any point in time, no matter how comfortable some given point may seem. And if love and commitment cannot allow growth and accompanying vulnerability for the sake of change, then that relationship will die.

This brings us full circle again to the need for

trust, and not security. All these things are related and nurture one another. Trust, freedom, and growth are the marks of God's covenant commitment to us, and they should be our goals in covenant with one another.

There is a final word that must be said. It is a word about broken covenant in relationship. Covenants do get broken, and the divorced are among the most hidden and marginal in our congregational life. Their issues are among the least cared for in the life of the church.

In the Old Testament, covenant is associated with life, and broken covenant is associated with death. This is what the divorced often experience. Grief over a death, the death of a relationship. The divorced are grieving persons, experiencing loss and the pain that accompanies that loss. The church, tragically, often leaves them alone in that grief. The responses to the divorced in our congregations range from silence to embarrassment to antagonism and seldom any farther. Those wounded and broken persons are wounded further by our refusal to deal caringly with their woundedness.

Our faith story is not one in which brokenness has the final word. Our faith story is a story in which life has a further word to speak beyond the reality of death. We so often want the resurrection without the crucifixion. We want somehow to speak a word of life without acknowledging the grip of death in the many forms that people experience. Our faith is one which says that, against the reality of death, life has a further word to speak. God's steadfast love endures forever, but over and over again we will experience in many different forms the pain of broken covenant.

We need to know that God is not only the covenant maker, but the covenant renewer. Beyond a broken covenant is God's forgiveness and redemption and the steadfast love of God, which renews broken covenants, which restores broken relationship. This too should model the church's activity toward those who are themselves experiencing broken relationships to one another. Beyond our broken covenants are possibilities for forgiveness and redemption. The church must actively proclaim this Good News. Why have we forgotten, in this arena, that nothing separates us from the love of God? God's forgiveness and renewal are unconditional.

Once again God's forgiveness models the forgiveness we must practice. Our tendency is to think of forgiveness as something we do for the other person, and the result is often patronizing. Listen to this passage from Isaiah 43:25 where God speaks to sinful Israel in exile:

> I, I am the one,
>   who blots out your transgressions
>   for my own sake.
>   I will remember your sins no more.
>   (author's trans.)

Isn't that interesting? God's forgiveness is for God's own sake. What we should begin to learn from this is that the church forgives and renews, not as something patronizing we do for the other, but as something we must do for ourselves, out of our need for restored relationship. Our willingness to "remember no more" and to seek the new is not a favor we do others but the way in which we claim our own calling as the church of Jesus Christ. We are called to offer forgiveness and reconciliation without condition as God has already done for us.

Only recently, I was in a Bible study where a part of the subject was the parable of the prodigal son. The leader of the study asked us a very interesting question. He said, "Okay, we've talked about all the various dynamics of the prodigal son. Here's a hypothetical situation: If you were a father at the end of this parable, how would you take all that you possess and redivide it between the two sons?" The first and immediate response in the group was made by a pastor who blurted out, "No way! There has to be some consequence for sin!" But is this parable not about forgiveness? It is an intriguing question, is it not? When will we learn from God that it is for our own sake as the church that we must learn to forgive, to forget those places where we think we as the church have been wounded, so that we may genuinely minister to the wounded among us?

It often seems that in the case of the broken relationships of divorce, the church thinks *it* has suffered the deepest wounds. Nothing separates us from the love of God. We are called to covenant relationship, but we will experience brokenness as well. Nevertheless, we are redeemed for *shalom*, for the wholeness God intended in creation, and the wholeness God constantly seeks in relationship to us and the world.

CHAPTER 4

Relationship as Wholeness

*I*n this final chapter we must speak about relationship as *shalom*. In the Bible, the goal of all relationships is to be *shalom*. God's relationship to us, our relationship to one another, our relationship to our own selves, and our relationship to the whole of creation are all relationships to be characterized by *shalom*.

Beyond the common and ordinary use of *shalom* as a word meaning "peace," there is a broader foundational understanding to this term which means "wholeness." *Shalom* is a Hebrew word that has as its basic meaning "wholeness," and it is a word that suggests and puts forward a vision so comprehensive that it encompasses all of those things that make for wholeness, and therefore, move us toward the vision of *shalom*. Peace, justice, well-being, wholeness, health, righteousness: all of these things participate in the vision of the reality of *shalom*.

Walter Brueggemann describes the meaning of *shalom* like this:

> The central vision of world history in the Bible is that all of creation is one, every creature in

community with every other, living in harmony and security toward the joy and well-being of every other creature.[1]

Shalom is best understood when we as human beings experience wholeness and harmony with God, with self, with others, and with creation. That vision appears from first to last in the biblical material, Old Testament and New Testament. It is one of the most comprehensive biblical symbols we have.

Shalom is God's intent in creation in the first place. As we noted in chapter 1, God created us for wholeness, as part of an interrelated world. When any are denied their full participation in the creation of God, we are all thereby diminished. In the human community, when any are broken, denied their full humanity, we are all less than human. When any part of our humanness, such as our sexuality, is denied full worth as a part of our created wholeness, then we are denying the wholeness God intended.

We live in an age that often suggests we can seek self-fulfillment as if that were an isolated concern. *Shalom* has something to do with wholeness of the self. *Shalom* does relate to that sense of oneness, unity, and harmony that we experience when we can affirm our worth as full human beings—but not as an end in itself, and not in isolation from other selves. Self-fulfillment is never a goal in and of itself. The wholeness we experience as self must be experienced in com-

munity with other selves in the interrelatedness
that God intended for creation.

Shalom also appears as the goal of covenant
community. It is a vision not only in the creation
material, but also in the testimony to a community of faith called into covenant relationship with
God. *Shalom* is the goal that covenant community seeks to embody and make possible in the
world. When divine covenant love is returned
by our righteousness, and justice, and faithful-
ness, then *shalom* is made present. The task of
covenant community is to seek constantly to
embody that *shalom* in the structures of faithful
community life, making *shalom* visible in structures that create wholeness. Thus, those who
work on issues of human relationship should
understand clearly from the biblical material that
they are working not only in the realm of personal
dimensions of relationship, but also in the social
realities of public policy, and the structures of
community life that either make *shalom* possible, or settle for brokenness. We should not think
that we can deal in the interpersonal without
dealing with the social realities where we live out
those interpersonal relationships.

In the Bible the stories of Israel and of the early
church all reflect the efforts and sometimes the
struggles of the covenant communities of faith to
embody *shalom* in their own lives and to make
shalom visible in the world around them.
Sometimes they fail in this task, but overall it is
the biblical communities in their efforts to

embody *shalom* in the concrete structures of their personal and social lives that keep God's *shalom* vision visible in an otherwise broken world.

This structuring of *shalom* in faithful community, and God's redemptive work calling that community into being, are made necessary by the brokenness of *shalom*. We have talked about creation, and the vision of wholeness for which we were created. We have talked about our own sexuality as part of that vision of God's wholeness. But we all know that we live in a broken world. Wholeness is not the reality that we always find. If *shalom* is the vision that stands before us, brokenness is the reality that often confronts us.

The brokenness of *shalom* is what the biblical material talks about as sin. Sin points to all forms of brokenness experienced in human relationship. But it has been common to suggest that sin is more applicable to some areas of human relationship than to others. For example, sin has often been the primary category used in some quarters of the church to talk about our human sexuality. Conversely, the church has been reluctant to speak boldly about sin in relation to child and spouse abuse for fear of invading the area of family relationships, where it has been easier to speak of ideals of wholeness than the realities of brokenness which sometimes exist.

We could talk at length about the biblical understanding of sin. There are many different

categories through which the materials of the
Scripture speak of the realities of sin. Sin is pride.
Sin is unbelief. Sin is rebellion. Sin is self-
centeredness. Sin is self-rejection. Sin is disobedience. There are many different ways of talking
about sin, but what we have not understood is that
all these ways of talking about sin have one thing
in common. All understandings of sin are simply
ways of talking about how *shalom* gets broken.
When *shalom* is broken, when wholeness is not
present, when we are not experiencing harmony
with God, with others, and with creation itself, we
are participating in the reality of sin.

To understand sin in this way is to divert
ourselves from our preoccupation with sins as the
listing of moral transgressions (as if we could make
a complete list) to a concern for sin as the condition
of brokenness we all experience. Sometimes we are
so preoccupied with listing our favorite individual
moral concerns that we fail to see the way in which
the brokenness we experience between one another is the sin in which we *all* participate. Sin is a
condition, and not an act.

When we fail to understand that we all
participate in the sinful condition of brokenness,
we are tempted to make lists of sins that are more
grievous than others. This is a response more
appropriate to the Pharisees than to the community called into being by the life, ministry, and death
of Jesus Christ. In his associations with many of
those considered outcasts and sinners, he con-
fronted the Pharisees with their self-righteousness.

To see sin as the brokenness of *shalom* is to turn from blame to reconciliation. To see sin in this way is not to ask, Who has done something wrong? but to ask, How can brokenness be made whole? In no area is this understanding of sin as broken *shalom* more needed than in the issues of human relationship and especially human sexuality. In this area, the church, rather than focus on the condition of brokenness which divides us from one another and from our full humanity, and which we all experience together, has been constantly prone to pointing fingers and listing sins. If we are divided in the church on issues of human sexuality, then we must spend more effort discovering what makes for wholeness in human relationship, including our sexuality, and less time labeling some viewpoints or persons as sinful.

In recent years many church bodies have been torn by divisions over issues of human sexuality. Some would like to ignore these issues, but we cannot deny the reality of that broken condition as if the issues do not exist, and still be faithful to our calling to seek *shalom*. Some would like to put these issues aside by majority vote, but *shalom* cannot be restored just by commanding it so in rules, moralisms, and legislation. To deal with sin as the broken relationships we all experience requires the church to take up the task of seeking those paths that will lead us toward wholeness even in the midst of our difficult divisions and brokenness.

We also avoid speaking of sin because it has frequently been confused with guilt. Nothing could be farther from the biblical testimony. Recognizing our sin, our lack of *shalom*, does not call us to guilt. Over and over again this has been a fundamental confusion in the life of the church. What we are called to is not guilt, but repentance. Guilt always looks backward in regret at what cannot be changed. So guilt is always static. It goes nowhere. But the biblical word for repentance is the simple Hebrew verb "to turn" (*shuv*). It means to turn and go in another direction. It is forward-looking, creative; it moves into the future, claims new possibilities for life over against the realities of brokenness. Brokenness cannot be allowed to go unchallenged with no vision of wholeness, but guilt never gets us there. Repentance is the fundamental resolve, when we catch sight of that vision, to turn and move toward it. The Good News of the gospel *frees us from guilt*, but *calls us to repentance*.

If we live in a broken world, as I believe we do, and if we experience that brokenness in our own selves, in our relationships to others, in the relationships we see being acted out in the communities of which we are a part, how do we respond to the need for *shalom*? What moves us toward that vision? What keeps us from just giving up in discouragement? Some people are simply settling for survival, because they do not have any wider vision. That mentality, in biblical terms, is an "exile" mentality.

There is an important word for the church, to be claimed in reflection on Israel's experience of the Babylonian Exile. We have seldom contemplated the message of that experience of exile for us as people of faith in the modern world. Somehow it seems like such a negative theme. After all, it was the biggest catastrophe and disaster in the whole story of Israel. It is, however, an important story for us to contemplate because it is finally a story of how hope can be claimed in the midst of brokenness—how broken *shalom* is made whole again.

The basic facts of the historical experience were these: In 587 B.C.E., a Babylonian army broke through the walls of Jerusalem. Jerusalem's leadership had arrogantly held out to the last moment believing that God would protect them as a privileged people. It was their flagrant disregard for justice and righteousness, the greedy materialism of the wealthy and powerful, and the willful disregard of their covenant with God that had finally brought this fate upon them. It was Jeremiah who tried to warn them. He preached against those who "have treated the wound of my people carelessly, saying, 'Peace, peace,' when there is no peace" (*Shalom, shalom,* when there is no *shalom.* Jeremiah 6:14; 8:11). But to the end, Jerusalem's leaders believed that religion was a matter of privileged position rather than of obedience. Instead of seeking *shalom* as their mission, they demanded it as their right, and in return brought only brokenness.

A Babylonian army finally broke through the walls of Jerusalem, tore the walls down stone from stone, destroyed the Temple, ended the Davidic kingship, and carried all the chief citizens of the land away into exile (2 Kings 25:1-21).

This experience was more than a matter of geography (some Jews were carried off to live in another place). This was an overturning of all those seemingly secure centers of meaning in the life of that people. All of the things they counted on to secure and anchor meaning in their world were overturned and thrown into confusion. Exile is the time when the things we thought we could count on are called into question.

Listen again to Psalm 137:

By the rivers of Babylon
    there we sat down and there we wept
      when we remembered Zion.
On the willows there
    we hung up our harps.
For there our captors
    asked us for songs,
and our tormentors asked for mirth, saying,
    "Sing us one of the songs of Zion!"
How could we sing the Lord's song
    in a foreign land?

The implied answer to that question is, We can't sing the song! That is what exile is all about. It is when the songs will not come. The secure centers of our lives have been thrown into chaos and confusion, and we cannot find the melody of the Lord's song any longer.

Exile is an important image for the modern church, because it characterizes the many areas of uncertainty and confusion that grip us in this world of ours. We live in an age when many settle for life lived in the present moment because the future is unclear. Economic recession, crime in cities and suburbs, homelessness, the threats and realities of global conflict, continuing racism, the lure of material life-styles, environmental damage, changing patterns of family life, substance abuse, the economic pressures of an aging population—all of these issues and others contribute to a sense of exile. We settle for survival and live for the moment, and the songs of hope in God's future, our own future, do not come easily.

Exile is indeed an image that affects all the areas of our lives, and it is an image important in dealing with the issues and concerns of human relationship and sexuality. We live in a time when there is extreme uncertainty and confusion over roles, behaviors, values, and cultural patterns. Family and relationship patterns have changed and are under pressures unimagined even a generation ago. On these matters there are as yet no clear songs coming from the church, and many in the church choose not to sing at all (to leave these issues unaddressed) because the song to sing is unclear.

We do not bring up the issues of exile simply to

end our study on a gloomy note. Here is a remarkable thing about the biblical testimony to the exile experience. In the midst of one of the most devastating sets of circumstances in all of Israel's experience, there arise some of the most eloquent voices of hope in the entire Scripture, the great hopeful voices of Jeremiah, Deutero-Isaiah, and Ezekiel. They are singers of God's song in the community of nonsingers, telling us something about what it might mean to give the church a few singing lessons.

Jeremiah wrote a letter to the exiles (Jeremiah 29). Among other things, he says to the exiles there, "Seek the *shalom* of the city where I have sent you . . . for in its *shalom*, you will find your *shalom.*" This is usually translated in English Bibles "Seek the welfare of the city where I have sent you . . . for in its welfare you will find your welfare" (29:7). This is an extraordinarily important word to the church in our own exile time, a time with much confusion and uncertainty over our ability to sing the Lord's song. Jeremiah's word tells us that we have to deal with the realities we have been given and not wish for another set of realities, as if we could turn the clock back to a previous era. That admonition would certainly affect how the church deals with issues of human relationship! Jeremiah's word calls us to free ourselves in those discussions from nostalgia for a reality that does not exist anymore in order to deal faithfully and forthrightly with the difficult issues involved in seeking

God's *shalom* in our human relationships, in-cluding the issues related to our human sexuality.

Another voice out of the exile, the anonymous prophet we call only Deutero-Isaiah or Second Isaiah, gives us the most eloquent testimony to hope in the scriptures. In the midst of the nonsingers by the rivers in Babylon comes the prophetic voice, saying, "Sing to the Lord a new song" (Isaiah 42:10). He opens his message with those well-known words in Isaiah 40:1-2 (RSV), "Comfort, comfort my people, says your God. Speak tenderly to Jerusalem, and cry to her that her warfare is ended, that her iniquity is pardoned." It is wonderfully appropriate that in the midst of the nonsingers in Babylon, there comes a prophet whose opening words are probably better known to us in Handel's musical setting *(Messiah)* than in any other way.

This prophet is a prophet who, in the midst of those who have given up vision, rekindles vision in remarkable, hopeful, and imaginative terms. But at the same time, he grounds that vision in a reclaiming of the faith tradition available as a resource of hope.

> Look to the rock from which you were hewn,
>   and to the quarry from which you were dug.
> Look to Abraham your father
>   and to Sarah who bore you.
>
> (Isaiah 51:1*b*-2*a*)

Memory and vision become the fertile soil out of which hope grows.

This prophet, beginning with a word of comfort, ends with these words,

> For you shall go out in joy,
>   and be led back in peace *[shalom]*;
> the mountains and the hills before you
>   shall burst into song,
>   and all the trees of the field shall clap
>   their hands.
>
> (Isaiah 55:12)

If you cannot sing, then God's creation will still sing around you. Join in. Claim the song. Sing to the Lord a new song. What would it mean for the church to become the singer of a new song in the midst of the exile we experience in dealing with the difficult and challenging issues of our own relationships? What could we offer as *shalom* in the area of this brokenness? The prophet suggests that we will find it by reclaiming our own traditions while yet daring to see new visions, and that this will be possible because God is still at work creating the possibilities of *shalom*.

If we need a song to sing in the midst of the brokenness we experience in our relationships, then we already have an example in the biblical material, and wonderfully it is called "Song of Songs." Why is it not sung more often? Song of Songs is poetry in celebration of the wondrous gift of human love and sexuality. To claim it anew is

to teach ourselves once again to sing of our love
and sexuality as *shalom*, to claim the wholeness
of our relational and sexual being. Listen to just a
few excerpts:

> The voice of my beloved!
>   Look, he comes,
> leaping upon the mountains,
>   bounding over the hills.
> My beloved is like a gazelle,
>   or a young stag.
> Look, there he stands
>   behind our wall,
> gazing in at the windows,
>   looking through the lattice.
> My beloved speaks and says to me:
> "Arise, my love, my fair one,
>   and come away;
> for now the winter is past,
>   the rain is over and gone.
> The flowers appear on the earth;
>   the time of singing has come,
> and the voice of the turtledove
>   is heard in our land.
> The fig tree puts forth its figs,
>   and the vines are in blossom;
>   they give forth fragrance.
> Arise, my love, my fair one,
>   and come away
>
> . . . .
>
> Let me see your face,
>   let me hear your voice;
> for your voice is sweet,
>   and your face is lovely."
>
> . . . .

My beloved is mine and I am his;
  he pastures his flock among the lilies.
Until the day breathes
  and the shadows flee,
turn, my beloved, be like a gazelle
  or a young stag on the cleft mountains.

                             (2:8-17)

Set me as a seal upon your heart,
  as a seal upon your arm;
for love is strong as death,
  passion fierce as the grave

. . . .

Many waters cannot quench love,
  neither can floods drown it.
If one offered for love
  all the wealth of his house,
  it would be utterly scorned.

                             (8:6-7)

This is poetry in celebration of human love and sexuality. It is poetry that bespeaks the *shalom* of our createdness as human and sexual beings. With its rich language of wholeness, and its lush imagery of creation, many have come to believe that the Song of Songs was written to reclaim the Garden vision broken in Genesis 3. It is a renewal of the imagery of that initial creation with its harmony in all aspects of the created order. In the Song of Songs we find the *shalom* vision reclaimed anew as the purpose of God's redemptive work in a world that has become broken, but in which God continually puts forward the vision of our wholeness.

Let us turn to a final New Testament image. How is *shalom* restored? For Christians, Jesus Christ is the fulfillment and the embodiment of *shalom*. In him, that which was broken is made whole, and that which was divided is reunited. It is appropriate that we should refer to Jesus by the title of Isaiah 9, "Prince of Peace" (Prince of *Shalom*). Just as *shalom* first appears in God's creation, so it is now restored in Jesus Christ as new creation. We, as the church, are called to be the community of that new creation.

Let us listen to a passage from Ephesians 2:13-17, in which the language of *shalom* is explicitly claimed as the meaning of Jesus Christ. In this passage the word for peace, of course, now appears in the Greek, but behind that Greek word still stands the Hebrew understanding of *shalom* in the early Jewish-Christian community:

> But now in Christ Jesus you who once were far off have been brought near by the blood of Christ. For he is our peace; in his flesh he has made both groups into one and has broken down the dividing wall, that is, the hostility between us. He has abolished the law with its commandments and ordinances, that he might create in himself one new humanity in place of the two, thus making peace, and might reconcile both groups to God in one body through the cross, thus

putting to death that hostility through it. So he
came and proclaimed peace to you who were far
off and peace to those who were near.

If Jesus Christ is our peace, then modeled for us
here in this passage is something of a word about
how we seek *shalom* in all of the areas of our
lives. Here is a word to us about those who seek
shalom and wholeness in human relationships.
Who are those far off who need to be brought near
just as Christ made *shalom* in bringing the far off
near? divorced persons? couples living together
outside marriage? single parents? blended families? victims of rape and abuse? gays and lesbians?
elderly persons stereotyped as nonsexual? teen-
agers bombarded with sexual imagery and ad-
monished with moralisms? those with AIDS?
Who are the far off who need to be brought near?
What are the dividing walls of hostility that
separate us? the dividing wall of our treatment of
sex as forbidden subject? the dividing wall of
moralisms and legalisms as substitute for dis-
cernment and decision? the dividing wall of
excluding those not like ourselves? The *shalom*
of Jesus Christ is to bring the far off near, to break
down the dividing walls of hostility.

The *shalom* of Jesus Christ is incarnational. As
the word was made flesh in Jesus Christ, we, too,
are called upon to embody, in the flesh, the vision
of shalom and this means physical presence in the
midst of the world's divisions. Why are the wards
of hospitals treating AIDS victims so often empty

of caring ministry? Why do we do so little in the church about child and spouse abuse? Why are so few single adults on church membership roles? What would it mean for us to be present in the midst of the world's divisions related to the issues of human relationship? It may place the church in some places it is not often found.

But the *shalom* of Jesus Christ is also cruci-form. Thus, if we are to make *shalom* as Christ has made *shalom*, it will be to take up our cross. If we take incarnation seriously we will be risking woundedness. The risk of the cross is a real risk, not an imaginary one. To take up the cross requires becoming vulnerable to the pain of the world whenever we encounter it. It requires a willingness to die, a willingness to be wounded for the sake of a wounded world. Jesus Christ is our peace. In him, those who were far off are brought near. In him, the dividing walls of hostility are broken down.

Phyllis Trible says she fantasizes that outside the garden of the Song of Songs is an angel with a flaming sword, like the one outside Eden. But the one outside Eden was there to keep people away from the experience of creation, which was lost because of brokenness. She fantasizes that the angel outside the garden of the Song of Songs is there to protect our experience of wholeness, the wholeness for which we were created. The angel is there to protect the garden of our wholeness by keeping out all "those who lust, moralize, legislate, or exploit."[2]

These seem to me to be good measures of faithful biblical understandings of relationships, which include our human sexuality, a sexuality that, as we have suggested in these studies, can be claimed in relationships of freedom, vulnerability, fidelity, and wholeness. We are a people who choose to live toward the vision of *shalom* in all of our being, in all of our relationships. When we know the beauty and the fullness of that vision, we should not be surprised that the community of faith has so often chosen to close its gatherings with the words I choose to close these studies, the words of Aaron's blessing in Numbers 6:24-26:

May the Lord bless you and keep you.
May the Lord's face shine upon you
   and be gracious to you.
May the Lord lift up the divine countenance upon
      you,
   and give you *shalom*. Amen.

(author's trans.)

REFLECTION QUESTIONS

*T*o assist groups who wish to use this book for adult study, following are two Bible readings provided for the theme of each chapter, and two questions to stimulate thinking about those texts. These texts and questions are intended as a stimulus and not an exhaustive treatment of the four themes. The readings and questions are best used in preparation for the chapters themselves, which will range over a much wider selection of biblical material. After reading the chapter, further discussion of its contents will build on the initial discussion of the two biblical texts.

CHAPTER 1: RELATIONSHIP AS FREEDOM

Read Genesis 1:26-28; Luke 15:11-32.

Relationship to God comes as a freely given gift. We are created for relationship, to God and to others, but it must be freely chosen and not coerced or legislated.

1. How do you understand creation in the

image of God? What does it mean to see that this includes both maleness and femaleness? What does this text imply about relationship as a part of our createdness?

2. How do you react to the story of the prodigal son? Think of it as a story of duty and grace, bondage and freedom. With whom do you identify in the story? Who in the story reflects your own experience of relationship?

CHAPTER 2: RELATIONSHIP AS VULNERABILITY

Read Exodus 3:7-8; Romans 8:31-39.

God chooses to participate in the human experience by experiencing with us our pain and suffering. God becomes vulnerable even to the point of death on the cross. God's love becomes visible in our midst.

1. How is God's vulnerability to be reflected in our relationships to one another? How are we to "know" one another and experience the deepest levels in our relationships? What are the risks of this "knowing" suggested in the text?

2. Does the unconditional character of God's love have a parallel in our relationships? What most threatens to separate us from the possibility of loving relationships?

CHAPTER 3: RELATIONSHIP AS FIDELITY

Read Genesis 38:1-30; John 7:53–8:11.

God's steadfast love endures forever. But it is

characterized by righteousness in the context of covenant relationship. We too often rigidify the concepts of righteousness, fidelity, and covenant in a manner more characteristic of the Pharisees' legalism than the covenant understanding of Moses' time or the teaching of Jesus.

1. In the story of Tamar, how do you respond to Judah's remarkable statement about Tamar's righteousness? Does this suggest changes in your concept of righteousness regarding human relationships?

2. Do covenant and law include room for grace in your understanding? How do we as a church read the gospel story in John? Does grace rule out accountability? Think of the parable of the prodigal son we read for chapter 1 as a story of forgiveness. Can we forgive as readily as the father in this parable?

CHAPTER 4: RELATIONSHIP AS WHOLENESS

Read Jeremiah 29:1-7; Ephesians 2:13-18.

Shalom means wholeness and encompasses all that makes for wholeness. It was for *shalom* that God created us, and *shalom* is the goal of the faith community. *Shalom* is then also the goal of our relationships, and all that we do in relationship should be measured in terms of its capacity for wholeness.

1. In Jeremiah 29, the word translated "welfare" in most versions (v. 7) is the Hebrew word *shalom*. What then does it mean to "seek the

shalom [wholeness] of the city where I have sent you . . . for in its *shalom* you will find your *shalom* ''? Has the church faced realistically the world where it finds itself when it considers concerns of relationship, particularly in the area of human sexuality? What would it mean to seek the welfare of our present world rather than wishing for a set of circumstances no longer ours?

2. *Shalom* is the concept behind the Greek word for peace in Ephesians 2. What are the walls of hostility that divide us in the area of human relationship? Who are the far off and how are they to be brought near? How has Jesus Christ modeled *shalom* for us in these areas?

NOTES

CHAPTER 2: RELATIONSHIP AS VULNERABILITY

1. This is Phyllis Trible's phrase for representing the close connection the Hebrew terms suggest between humanity and the earth. *God and the Rhetoric of Sexuality* (Philadelphia: Fortress Press, 1978), pp. 75ff.

2. James A. Wharton, "Theology and Ministry in the Hebrew Scriptures," *A Biblical Basis for Ministry* (Philadelphia: Westminster Press, 1981), pp. 27-28.

3. Trible, *God and the Rhetoric of Sexuality*, pp. 31-59.

CHAPTER 4: RELATIONSHIP AS WHOLENESS

1. Walter Brueggemann, *Living Toward a Vision: Biblical Reflections on Shalom* (New York: United Church Press, 1976), p. 15.

2. Phyllis Trible, *God and the Rhetoric of Sexuality* (Philadelphia: Fortress Press, 1978), p. 162.

DATE DUE

11
B
Birch, Bruce C.

To Love as We are Loved

1348

DATE	ISSUED TO

1348

11
B   To Loved as We Are Loved

Birch, Bruce C